NOAH Builds an Ark

Coloring Book

Based on Genesis 6:9—9:17

Written by Robin Loisch

Illustrated by Mary Rojas

warner press KiDs

3058002100000525

Noah was a good man.
He loved God and obeyed Him.

**God said, "Noah, build an ark.
I am sending a flood to cover the earth."**

Noah obeyed God. He built the ark just like God told him to do.

God said, "Bring a male and a female of every animal into the ark."

The animals came two by two.

Two of every kind of bird came.

The creatures that crawled along the ground came too.

God told Noah to bring plenty of food. Noah, his family, and all the animals would be on the ark for a long time.

**At last, Noah and his wife entered the ark.
Noah's three sons and their wives came too.
When everyone was on the ark, God shut the door.**

For 40 days and 40 nights, the rain came down.
The water rose so high it covered the whole earth.

Noah, his family, and all the animals were safe on the ark.

After many days, God sent the wind to dry up the water. The ark stopped on top of a mountain.

Twice, Noah sent out a dove to see if the land was dry yet. The second time the dove brought back an olive leaf.

God told Noah it was time to leave the ark.

Noah thanked God. God promised He would never flood the whole earth again. Then God put a beautiful rainbow in the sky to remind us of His promise.